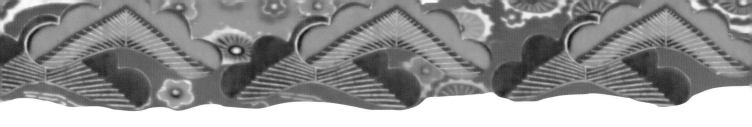

COSTUME AROUND THE WORLD
Japan

Jane Bingham

CHELSEA
CLUBHOUSE
An Imprint of Chelsea House Publishers

Copyright © 2008 Bailey Publishing Associates Ltd

Produced for Chelsea Clubhouse by Bailey Publishing Associates Ltd
11a Woodlands, Hove BN3 6TJ
England

Project Manager: Roberta Bailey
Editor: Alex Woolf
Text Designer: Jane Hawkins
Picture Research: Roberta Bailey and Shelley Noronha

Chelsea Clubhouse
An imprint of Chelsea House Publishers
132 West 31st Street
New York NY 10001

ISBN 978-0-7910-9770-0

Library of Congress Cataloging-in-Publication Data
Costume around the world.—1st ed.
     v. cm.
     Includes bibliographical references and index.
     Contents: [1] China / Anne Rooney—[2] France / Kathy Elgin—[3] Germany / Cath Senker—[4] India / Kathy Elgin—[5] Italy / Kathy Elgin—[6] Japan / Jane Bingham—[7] Mexico / Jane Bingham—[8] Saudi Arabia / Cath Senker—[9] Spain / Kathy Elgin—[10] United States / Liz Gogerly.
     ISBN 978-0-7910-9765-6 (v. 1)—ISBN 978-0-7910-9766-3 (v. 2)—ISBN 978-0-7910-9767-0 (v. 3)—ISBN 978-0-7910-9768-7 (v. 4)—ISBN 978-0-7910-9769-4 (v. 5)—ISBN 978-0-7910-9770-0 (v. 6)—ISBN 978-0-7910-9771-7 (v. 7)—ISBN 978-0-7910-9773-1 (v. 8)— ISBN 978-0-7910-9772-4 (v. 9)—ISBN 978-0-7910-9774-8 (v. 10) 1. Clothing and dress—Juvenile literature.
     GT518.C67 2008
     391—dc22   2007042756

Chelsea Clubhouse books are available at special discounts when purchased in bulk quantities for businesses, associations, institutions, or sales promotions. Please call our Special Sales Department in New York at (212) 967-8800 or (800) 322-8755.

You can find Chelsea Clubhouse on the World Wide Web at: http://www.chelseahouse.com

Printed and bound in Hong Kong

10 9 8 7 6 5 4 3 2 1

The publishers would like to thank the following for permission to reproduce their pictures:
Chris Fairclough Worldwide Ltd: 4, 11, 21, 24, 28
Corbis: 6 (Nik Wheeler), 9 (Everett Kennedy Brown/epa), 18 (Alison Wright), 20 (Everett Kennedy Brown/epa)
Empics: 25 (Kamran Jebreili/AP/PA Photos)
Rex Features: 8 and title page (Roy Garner), 23 (A. Shilo/Israel), 26 (Richard Jones)
Topfoto: 5, 7, 10 (Image Works), 12 (Alinari), 13 (AP), 14 (Alinari),15, 16, 17, 19, 22 , 27 (Image Works), 29
Victoria and Albert Museum: decorative borders

Contents

Costumes of Japan 4

Japan Past and Present 6

Rocks, Trees, and Water 8

Religion and Tradition 10

Textiles, Dyeing, and Weaving 12

Traditional Dress 14

Clothes for Special Occasions 16

The Well-Dressed Man 18

The Well-Dressed Woman 20

Clothes for Work 22

Clothes for Sports 24

Important Extras 26

International Style 28

Glossary 30

Further Information 31

Index 32

Costumes of Japan

Japan is a fascinating country. It lies close to China, in the Pacific Ocean, and it is made up of more than 3,000 islands. Most of Japan's people live on just four islands: Hokkaido, Honshu, Shikoku, and Kyushu. The capital city, Tokyo, is on Honshu, the largest island.

A country of contrasts

Japan is a land of contrasts. On the small islands and in country areas, people have a quiet, unhurried way of life. Here many people wear the same sort of clothes that their ancestors did. In the cities, life is fast paced and busy. Japanese city dwellers usually wear modern, Western-style clothes. But even in the cities, there are times when people like to wear traditional dress.

In Japan's city streets, you can see modern clothes and traditional dress side by side.

Children love dressing up for the Schichi-go-san ceremony.

Children's traditions

Japanese children usually dress in modern clothes. However, they still wear traditional costumes for special occasions. At the Shichi-go-san (seven-five-three) ceremony, girls age three and seven and boys age five dress up in the kinds of clothes that children wore in the past.

Ancient traditions

The people of Japan have many ancient traditions. Throughout the year, there are ceremonies and festivals. Actors perform traditional plays, and there are several ancient sports, such as sumo wrestling, judo, and karate. For all of these activities, people wear special costumes.

A range of clothes

A range of clothes are worn in Japan. People dress in costumes from the past for traditional activities and have other kinds of clothes for everyday wear.

Japan Past and Present

The first people of Japan were the Jomon. They survived by fishing, hunting, and gathering food and wore simple clothes made from animal skins. The Jomon period came to an end in about 500 BCE, when settlers began to arrive from Korea and China.

At the hollyhock festival, modern men and women dress up in the costumes of the ancient emperors' court.

The emperor's court

Gradually, a tribe called the Yamato gained control of Japan, and in about 300 CE, a Yamato chief became Japan's first emperor. By the 700s, the emperor was living with his court in a beautiful palace. All the members of the emperor's court dressed in splendid robes.

Shoguns and samurai

By the 1000s, the emperors had lost most of their power and Japan was controlled by shoguns. The shoguns were military commanders who dressed in dark robes made from the finest silk. They relied on local lords, called samurai, to rule the different parts of the country. The shoguns ruled Japan for 700 years, and for most of this time, Japan had no contact with the outside world. However, in 1854, Japan made a trading agreement with the U.S. This was the start of a new period in Japanese history.

Japanese samurai wore heavy armor made from leather decorated with metal.

Into the modern world

In 1868, the emperor regained control of Japan and began to copy Western ideas. Many people began to wear Western-style clothes, and Japanese society changed dramatically.

Today Japan plays an important part in the modern world. It has many thriving industries, but its ancient past has not been forgotten.

Fashion dolls

In the 1700s, Japanese people began to make "fashion dolls." These dolls were dressed in the finest fashions from the emperor's court.

Rocks, Trees, and Water

Japan is a country of rocks, trees, and water. Mountains and forests cover about three-quarters of Japan's total area. There are also thousands of miles of rocky coastline.

Most people in Japan live on the lower slopes of the mountains or along the coast. Forestry, farming, and fishing have always been very important to the Japanese.

A varied climate

Summers in Japan are hot and humid, with lots of rain. Winters are very cold, with snow over the mountains. In the summer, many people wear light cotton robes known as *yukatas* (see page 16). In the winter, people in country areas often wear quilted clothes to keep themselves warm (see page 22).

Today, many women and girls wear a colorful *yukata* for a shopping trip.

8

Materials for clothes

By the 1900s, Japan had begun to import materials from other countries, but before that time, farmers grew all the materials they needed to make their clothes They grew flax for making linen and used other plants, such as jute and ramie, to make into coarser cloth. Simple rope sandals were made from plant fibers. Wood from trees was used to make wooden shoes called *geta*.

Cotton and silk

In the 1700s, some farmers in Japan began to grow cotton to make into clothes. Many Japanese farmers also kept silkworms. The silk that they produced was sold to merchants and made into clothes for the rich.

Workers in the fields often wear padded cotton clothes. These tea-pickers also have special gloves to protect their hands.

Geta and tabi

Geta are simple wooden shoes with a thong through the toes. They are raised above the ground on two wooden blocks so that people can walk on wet ground without getting their long robes dirty. *Geta* are worn with special socks called *tabi*. These white cotton socks have a split between the big toe and the rest of the toes.

Religion and Tradition

The people of Japan have many ancient beliefs. They also have traditions, such as the acting of Noh plays, that have stayed unchanged for hundreds of years.

A Shinto priest, dressed in his long silk robe, blesses children in an ancient ceremony.

Religious beliefs

The two main religions of Japan are Shinto and Buddhism. Followers of the Shinto faith gather at shrines to pray to the spirits of nature. Shinto priests usually wear a tall black hat and long silk robes dyed white, blue, or purple.

Buddhist monks and nuns live a very simple life dedicated to prayer and meditation. They dress in long robes colored with saffron, a dye that comes from the crocus flower. Robes dyed with saffron can be brown, red, orange, or yellow.

Noh plays

Noh plays combine singing, dancing, music, and poetry. The actors wear elaborate costumes made from silk and brocade (a stiff fabric with a raised design). They also wear masks that represent different characters, such as an old man, a beautiful woman, or a demon. Like the masks, Noh costumes have special meanings. For example, the actor playing a dragon wears a robe covered with triangles to represent the dragon's scales.

A Kabuki actor in his striking costume and makeup. Even his legs and feet are made up!

Kabuki makeup

Kabuki plays were first performed in the 1600s. They tell stories of passion and revenge, and Kabuki actors are famous for their striking costumes and makeup. Kabuki actors have white faces with dramatic lines drawn on them. The color of the lines shows an actor's character. Red lines show that the character is brave and good. Blue or black lines indicate evil. Green is the color of supernatural creatures, and purple is used for lords.

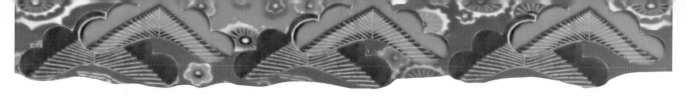

Textiles, Dyeing, and Weaving

Traditional Japanese clothes are made from a wide variety of materials. Satin and silk are used for the grandest robes, while cotton is the usual choice for summer clothing. Some clothes are made from plant fibers, and there are even textiles made from banana trees.

In the past, Japanese silk was woven on wooden looms. Now it is usually produced in factories.

Different dyes

Today Japanese cloth is usually colored with chemical dyes, but in the past, most dyes came from plants and minerals. One of the most popular dyes is a vivid blue made from the indigo plant. Indigo dye is still widely used in Japan today, but now it is made chemically. It produces a range of colors from pale blue to deep navy.

Using dyes

Japanese textiles are colored in many different ways. They may be dipped in different dyes to create several layers of color, or they may have dyes hand-painted onto them. Textile makers also create complex patterns using

12

wax-resist dyeing. They cover parts of the cloth with wax, then they dip it into the dye. The covered areas remain uncolored, creating a design on the cloth.

This many-layered wedding robe is dyed in traditional, natural colors and decorated with embroidered silk patterns.

Weaving and embroidery

The finest kimonos are made from richly patterned silk. Spectacular designs are woven into the cloth using silk and golden threads. Woven designs for kimonos often show flowers, trees, or birds.

Some kimonos are decorated with embroidery. Embroidered patterns and scenes can be very elaborate. They may include complex knots and tassels and even panels of gold leaf.

Kasuri weaving

The famous Japanese technique of *kasuri* weaving combines weaving and dyeing. First the weavers work out which parts of the thread should be dyed. Then they weave their pattern. The result is a soft, slightly fuzzy-looking pattern.

Traditional Dress

The most important garment in Japanese traditional costume is the kimono. This long, T-shaped robe was originally copied from the robes of the Chinese emperors, and the first kimonos had very long sleeves, reaching to the ground. However, by the 1000s, kimonos had become simpler in shape.

Many parts

Japanese kimonos are never worn on their own. They are just one part of an elaborate costume. Other important parts are the *nagajuban*, or undergarment for the kimono, and the wide belt, called the *obi*. Some formal women's costumes have as many as 12 different parts, including several undergarments.

Getting dressed

Getting dressed in traditional costume is very complicated because

In the past, wealthy Japanese women had servants to help them to dress and arrange their hair.

each part has to be worn and fastened in a special way. For example, the kimono must always be worn with the left side over the right and each undergarment must show a strip of color at the neck and sleeves. Very few young women today know how to wear a traditional costume. For special occasions, they usually rely on a professional dresser.

Wedding clothes

Many Japanese people still choose to wear traditional dress for weddings. The bride at a Shinto wedding wears a heavy, embroidered kimono and an elaborate, boat-shaped headdress decorated with flowers. The groom wears a black silk kimono and a pleated skirt called a *hakama*.

Changing name

The Japanese word *kimono* simply means "clothing." However, in the 1700s, people began to use the word in a different way. It became the name for the T-shaped robe that forms the main part of Japanese traditional dress.

Japanese brides look spectacular in their colorful kimonos and elaborate headdresses!

15

Clothes for Special Occasions

People in Japan still wear formal, traditional dress for ancient ceremonies, such as the tea ceremony. During the year, there are also many festivals, such as the famous celebration to welcome the spring. These events are great opportunities for people to dress up in stunning costumes.

These men and boys are dressed for a festival in matching *happi* coats.

Dress for festivals

Women and girls often wear a *yukata* for festivals. *Yukatas* are T-shaped robes, like kimonos, but they are much lighter and easier to wear and are usually made of cotton. *Yukatas* worn for festivals tend to be brightly colored and covered with a bold flower design.

Popular festival wear for men and boys is a *happi* coat and matching headband. *Happi* coats are short cotton jackets with printed designs. They are tied with a simple sash and are usually worn with wide cotton pants.

16

Tea ceremony

The ancient tea ceremony is a way of showing great respect to a guest. For this important ritual, the hostess dresses in a single-colored kimono, called an *iromuji*, and performs her part gracefully and calmly. Wearing a beautiful, formal costume is a vital part of the ceremony.

A hostess at a tea ceremony wears an *iromuji*—a plain kimono with a simple pattern.

Halloween

The Western celebration of Halloween has recently become very popular in Japan. It is seen as a chance to dress up in some very exciting, fancy costumes. Halloween costumes showing manga and Pokémon figures are especially popular.

Yukata and happi coats

Yukatas were originally worn by upper-class ladies after bathing, but later they became popular with ordinary people. *Happi* coats were traditionally worn by firemen and shopkeepers. Today these two garments are often bought as souvenirs by visitors to Japan.

The Well-Dressed Man

Many Japanese men today wear Western-style suits for formal occasions. However, some men still like to wear traditional dress, especially for weddings and funerals. Sumo wrestlers wear kimonos all the time, except when they are in the wrestling ring (see pages 24–25).

Some Japanese boys wear a kimono for special occasions. This boy is wearing a decorated kimono with a formal skirt, called a *hakama*.

Styles for men

Men's traditional costumes are simpler than women's, with a maximum of five separate pieces. Their kimonos are narrower than women's and have shorter sleeves.

Formal kimonos for men are mostly plain and dark in color, but the *nagajuban* (undergarment) provides the opportunity for brighter colors and patterns. Popular designs for a man's *nagajuban* are helmets, dragons, and rocky scenery.

Japanese men sometimes wear a casual kimono to visit friends. These casual kimonos may be light purple, green, or blue, and they may have a subtle pattern. For really casual occasions, some men choose to wear a colorful, patterned *yukata*.

Formal extras

For weddings and funerals, men usually wear a *hakama* (skirt) and *haori* (coat) with their kimono. The *hakama* is a pleated skirt that is sometimes divided in two, like very wide pants. *Hakamas* were originally worn by samurai warriors to protect their legs when they were riding horses. *Haoris* may reach to the hips or the thighs and were originally worn by the samurai.

Japanese formal dress for men has an interesting history. It is based on the costumes worn by the samurai warriors.

Family crests

Men's formal kimonos often feature a small family crest, embroidered in a circle. This crest, known as a *kamon*, is usually shown five times—on the chest, shoulders, and back. Many family crests date to the time of the shoguns and samurai.

Sumo shockers

Sumo wrestlers sometimes choose very bright colors for their kimonos, such as shocking pink!

The Well-Dressed Woman

Today most Japanese women wear Western dress, but they still enjoy looking elegant in traditional costumes. The *yukata* is the most popular form of traditional dress, but kimonos are often worn for special occasions.

A girl at the coming-of-age festival wears a colorful *furisode*.

Different kimonos

One occasion when all Japanese girls wear a kimono is their "coming-of-age" day. This festival is held in January for all the young people who will be 20 in the coming year. Girls wear the *furisode*, the costume traditionally worn by young, unmarried women. It has very long sleeves and is covered in colorful patterns.

When a married woman attends a formal occasion, she usually wears a *houmongi*—a kimono with patterns flowing over the shoulders and sleeves. For more casual events, such as visiting friends, women often choose the *komon*. This is less bulky than a formal kimono and is usually decorated with a small, repeated pattern.

Brilliant belts

The *obi* (belt) is a very important part of a woman's traditional dress. A formal woman's *obi* is made from a length of silk measuring about 13 feet (4 meters) long and 2 feet (60 centimeters) wide. This is folded in half, wrapped twice around the waist, and fastened with a complicated knot at the back. Sometimes extra padding is added to the knot, making a *makura*, or cushion, which is covered by an extra piece of silk. Finally, everything is held in place by a braided cord.

Married women usually wear less colorful kimonos, decorated with simple patterns.

Changing patterns

The patterns on women's kimonos change according to the time of the year. In spring, women's kimonos are decorated with butterflies and cherry blossoms. Autumn patterns show maple leaves, while winter kimonos have designs of pine trees and bamboo.

Clothes for Work

People in Japan wear a range of clothes to work. In the cities, office workers wear stylish business suits. In country areas, many people still wear simple traditional dress—a short cotton tunic and wide, loose pants, with a thick, quilted jacket in winter.

Quilted clothes

Until the 1900s, there were very few wool clothes in Japan, so people working outside wore quilted clothes to keep warm. These days, some people still make quilted clothes by stitching together many layers of material. They stitch traditional patterns, such as clouds or bamboo, into the clothes.

Uniforms for work

Today soldiers, police, and nurses in Japan all wear Western-style uniforms.

Japanese businessmen dress for work in Western-style suits.

22

Japanese firefighters wear flame-resistant suits, but a hundred years ago, they had a very distinctive uniform. Firefighters wore a padded hat with earflaps and a navy *happi* coat with a bold design in red and white on the back.

Chefs and construction workers

Japanese chefs in restaurants often wear a very tall, white hat. Sometimes they also wear extremely high *geta* (raised wooden sandals). Some chefs have *geta* that are raised 6 inches (15 centimeters) off the ground!

Japanese construction workers have bright yellow coveralls and very wide pants. They wear *jika tabi*—a kind of sock-shoe. *Jika tabi* look like Japanese *tabi* (cotton socks), but they have very thick rubber soles.

In Japan, even very young children wear school uniforms. These children are giving the peace sign.

School uniforms

Almost all schoolchildren in Japan wear a uniform. The most common uniform for girls is white shoes and long white socks, a navy blue skirt, and a sailor-style top with a very wide collar. Boys wear navy blue shorts or pants, a white shirt, and a tie.

Clothes for Sports

Japanese adults and children enjoy a wide variety of sports, including many ancient martial arts. They wear special costumes to practice their traditional sports.

Follow the fan

The referee in a sumo wrestling match carries a large wooden fan, which he uses to make special gestures at the contestants. This fan has its origins in samurai warfare, when the commander used a fan to give orders to his troops.

Sumo wresting

Sumo wrestlers wear a padded belt called a *mawashi*. It is made from about 30 feet (9 meters) of material, wrapped several times around the body and fastened at the back in a large knot. For practice sessions, wrestlers wear cotton *mawashi*, but for public contests, their belts are made from brightly colored silk.

Sumo wrestlers wear their embroidered "aprons" at the start of a contest. The aprons are removed before the fight begins.

In the opening ceremony of a sumo contest, wrestlers also wear an ornate, embroidered silk "apron," called a *kesho-mawashi*.

Kendo

Kendo is a kind of fencing in which contestants use sticks made from wood and bamboo. The sport has its origins in the duels fought by the samurai, and modern kendo costumes are based on the samurai's armor.

Contestants wear a short, black jacket, a long, pleated skirt (*hakama*), and four pieces of armor: a breastplate, a waist protector, gauntlets, and a helmet. The kendo helmet has wide shoulder pieces and is shaped like a samurai helmet.

Judo and karate

For the martial arts of judo and karate, contestants wear a simple suit of white or blue cotton. This suit consists of drawstring pants and a matching quilted jacket fastened by a belt. The color of the belt shows the wearer's level of skill: a white belt is the most junior rank and a black belt the most senior.

Judo and karate suits need to be light and easy to move in. These men are practicing karate.

Important Extras

Makeup, hairstyles, and accessories, such as matching bags, have always played a vital part in a traditional Japanese woman's costume. Even when they dress in Western-style clothes, Japanese women still pay a lot of attention to these important extras.

Bags, fans, and shoes

Women in traditional dress usually have a handbag made from the same material as their kimono. They may also carry a fan with a matching or contrasting pattern. When they are dressed in a kimono or a *yukata*, women usually wear *zori* and *tabi*—light sandals and socks. *Zori* are made from rice straw or lacquered wood.

Today fans are usually made from paper. In the past they were made from very thin strips of wood.

Hairstyles

In the past, some Japanese women had incredibly elaborate hairstyles. These styles were often decorated with flowers and held in place by beautiful combs and

hairpins made from jade, tortoiseshell, or wood. These days, hairstyles are much less fancy, but some young women and men have very striking geometric haircuts.

Geisha makeup

Geishas are hostesses who often entertain guests in teahouses. They are trained in traditional skills such as dancing, singing, and flower arrangement. Geishas are famous for their dramatic makeup, which has remained almost unchanged for hundreds of years. The geisha applies a thick, white base all over her face, black outline around her eyes and on her eyebrows, and bright red color on her lips. Traditionally, only a small area of the mouth was colored because tiny mouths were considered to be very attractive.

Beauty sleep

Some geisha hairstyles can take many hours to arrange. Before the 20th century, geishas were trained to sleep with their necks on wooden blocks so that they did not mess up their hair!

These Japanese geishas are wearing traditional makeup and hairstyles.

International Style

Japan plays a very important role in the world of international fashion. Japan's city stores sell all the latest styles, and Japanese designers set trends around the world.

Traditional fashions

Since the 1900s, Japanese fabrics, designs, and fashions have spread far beyond Japan. Traditional Japanese textiles, decorated with patterns of flowers, are very popular in Western countries. There has also been a growing demand for simple cotton fabrics printed with striking indigo designs.

Today many Westerners wear a simple version of the *yukata* as a light dressing gown. Clothes inspired by Japanese martial arts are also widely worn outside Japan.

Young people in Japan are very enthusiastic followers of fashion. They also like to set trends of their own!

28

This striking dress by Kenzo is clearly inspired by traditional Japanese costumes, with their many layers, patterns, and colors.

Modern trends

Japan has produced some of the world's leading fashion designers, such as Kenzo and Hanae Mori. Japanese fashion designs tend to be simple and bold. They usually have a very definite outline and often use a single, strong color, such as black. The simplified, dramatic style of many Japanese designs has had a very strong influence on international fashion.

Japanese brands

Recently, some Japanese clothing brands have enjoyed global success. *Muji* produces very simple clothes, such as pants and T-shirts, that are completely logo free. *Hello Kitty* started out as a cartoon character but soon became an international brand. Now the Sanrio company sells clothes and accessories to children and teenagers worldwide, along with a range of other products.

Platform shoes

Japan has always had traditional platform shoes—the *geta*. In the late 1990s, the practice of wearing platform shoes crossed over into fashion. Young Japanese women led the trend for extreme platform shoes, including sneakers with very thick rubber soles.

Glossary

brocade A stiff fabric with a raised design.

Buddhism A religion practiced mainly in eastern and central Asia.

embroidery Patterns or pictures stitched onto cloth.

furisode A type of kimono traditionally worn by young, unmarried women. The *furisode* has very long sleeves and is covered in colorful patterns.

gauntlets Long protective gloves. Gauntlets usually reach halfway up the arm.

geta Wooden-soled sandals with a thong between the toes, raised above the ground on two wooden blocks.

hakama A traditional, pleated skirt worn by Japanese men. The *hakama* is sometimes divided in two, like very wide pants.

haori A traditional coat worn by Japanese men. *Haoris* may reach to the hips or thighs.

happi **coat** A short cotton jacket worn by Japanese men and boys. *Happi* coats often have a bold printed design on the back.

houmongi A type of kimono traditionally worn by married women on formal occasions. The *houmongi* has patterns flowing over the shoulders and sleeves.

iromuji A single-colored kimono traditionally worn by women performing the tea ceremony.

jika tabi A kind of sock-shoe worn by some Japanese construction workers. *Jika tabi* look like *tabi* (cotton socks), but they have very thick rubber soles.

judo A traditional Japanese sport in which two people fight using controlled movements, and try to throw each other to the ground.

jute A stringy plant whose fibers are used for making coarse cloth or rope.

kamon A small family crest embroidered onto cloth in a circle.

karate A traditional Japanese sport in which two people fight using controlled movements, especially kicking with their feet and chopping with their hands.

kesho-mawashi An embroidered silk garment, like an apron, worn by sumo wrestlers in the opening ceremony of a contest.

kimono A long, T-shaped robe that is tied at the waist by a wide belt. Kimonos are worn by both Japanese men and women as part of their traditional dress.

komon A lightweight kimono that is usually decorated with a small, repeated pattern.

makura Padding added to the knot of a Japanese traditional belt to create a "cushion," which is covered by an extra piece of silk.

manga A Japanese style of comic-book illustration.

martial arts Sports that involve fighting with controlled moves and very strict rules.

mawashi A padded belt worn by sumo wrestlers.

meditation A kind of mental exercise designed to release the mind from its usual patterns of thinking.

nagajuban An undergarment worn under a kimono.

obi A wide belt used to fasten a kimono.

Pokémon "Pocket monster" characters, featured in Japanese computer games, comics, and toys.

quilted Padded with extra fabric, which is held in place by lines of sewing.

ramie A stringy plant whose fibers are used for making coarse cloth or rope.

ritual A set of actions that are always performed in the same way as part of a religious ceremony or a social custom.

samurai A Japanese warrior. The samurai lived in castles in Japan between the 1000s and 1800s.

Shinto The traditional religion of Japan. Followers of Shinto worship the spirits of nature.

shogun A Japanese military commander. The shoguns were very powerful in Japan from the 1000s to the 1800s.

tabi White cotton socks with a split between the big toe and the rest of the toes. *Tabi* are designed to be worn with sandals with thongs.

tea ceremony An ancient Japanese ceremony in which a hostess serves a guest with tea as a way of showing respect.

wax-resist dyeing A method of dyeing fabric in which parts of the cloth are covered with wax before it is dipped into the dye. The covered areas remain uncolored, creating a design.

yukata A light kimono, usually made of cotton.

zori Sandals with a thong between the toes. *Zori* are made from rice straw or lacquered wood.

Further Information

Books

Brownlie, Ali. *Letters from Around the World: Japan.* Cherrytree Books, 2006.

Fisher, Teresa. *We Come from Japan.* Raintree, 2000.

Guile, Melanie. *Culture in Japan.* Raintree, 2005.

Hammond, Paula. *Cultures and Costumes: Symbols of Their Period: China and Japan.* Mason Crest, 2003.

Tames, Richard and Sheila. *Country Topics: Japan.* Sea to Sea Publications, 2005.

Web sites

www.iz2.or.jp/english/
A well-illustrated Web site on the history of Japanese costume.

www.japanesekimono.com/
An illustrated guide to Japanese costume.

www.explorejapan.com/
A good general introduction to Japanese culture.

Index

Page numbers in **bold** refer to illustrations

accessories 26–27
aprons **24**, 25
armor 7, 25

belts 14, 21, 24, 25
brands 29
brocade 11, 30
Buddhist monks and nuns 11

children's clothes 5, **5**, **18**, 23, **23**, 29
city dress 4, **4**, 22
climate 8
coats 19
cotton 8, 9, 12, 16, 24, 25, 28
coveralls 23

decorative features 13, 21, 22, 26–27, 28
dresses **29**
dressing 14–15, **14**
dyes 11, 12–13

embroidery 13, 15, 19, **24**, 25, 30

fans 24, 26, **26**
fashion 28, 29, **29**
fashion dolls 7
festival costume 5, **6**, 16, **16**, 17, 20
funeral dress 18, 19
furisode 20, **20**, 30

geishas 27, **27**
geography 8
geta 9, 23, 29, 30
gloves **9**

hairstyles 26–27, **27**
hakama 15, **15**, 18, 19, 25, 30
Halloween 17
Hanae Mori 29
handbags 26
haori 19, 30

happi coat 16, **16**, 17, 23, 30
hats 10, 23
headbands 16
headdresses 15, **15**
helmets 25
history 6–7
houmongi 20–21, 30

iromuji 17, **17**, 30

jackets 16, 22, 25
jika tabi 23, 30
judo 5, 25, 30

Kabuki plays 11, **11**
kamon 19, 30
karate 5, 25, **25**, 30
kasuri weaving 13
kendo 25
Kenzo 29, **29**
kesho-mawashi **24**, 25, 30
kimono 13, 14, 15, **15**, 16, 17, 18, **18**, 19, 20, 21, **21**, 26, 30
komon 21, 30

linen 9

makeup 11, **11**, 26, 27, **27**
makura 21, 30
masks 11
mawashi 24, 30

nagajuban 14, 18, 30
Noh plays 11

obi 14, 21, 30

pants 16, 19, 22, 23, 25, 29
plant fibers 9, 12

quilted clothing 8, 22, 25

religion 10–11
robes 6, 7, 9, 10, **10**, 11, 12, **13**, 14, 15, 16
rural dress 4, 22

sailor-style tops 23
samurai 7, **7**, 19, **19**, 24, 25, 31

sandals 9, 23, 26
sashes 16
satin 12
school uniforms 23, **23**
Shichi-go-san 5, **5**
shirts 23
Shinto 10, 15, 31
Shinto priests 10, **10**
shoes 9, 23, 29
shorts 23
silk 7, 9, 10, 11, 12, **12**, 13, 15, 21, 24, 25
skirts 15, **18**, 19, 23, 25
sneakers 29
socks 9, 23, 26
sports clothing 24–25
suits **22**, 25
sumo wrestlers 5, 18, 19, 24, **24**

tabi 9, 23, 26, 31
tea ceremony 16, 17, **17**, 31
textiles 9, 12¬–13, 28
ties 23
traditional dress 4, **4**, 5, **5**, **6**, 14–15, **15**, 16–17, 18, 20, 21, 26
T-shirts 29
tunics 22

undergarments 14, 15

wax-resist dyeing 12–13, 31
weaving 13
wedding clothes 13, 15, **15**, 18, 19
Western-style clothes 4, **4**, 7, 18, 20, 22, **22**
wool 22
work uniforms 22–23

young people's clothing 28, 29
yukata 8, **8**, 16, 17, 19, 20, 26, 28, 31

zori 26, 31